T0129568

WOUNDED
BUT YET
WALKING

REBECCA E. McMILLAN

authorHOUSE®

AuthorHouse™
1663 Liberty Drive
Bloomington, IN 47403
www.authorhouse.com
Phone: 833-262-8899

Published by AuthorHouse 09/01/2020

ISBN: 978-1-7283-7135-1 (sc)
ISBN: 978-1-7283-7247-1 (e)

Library of Congress Control Number: 2020916582

Print information available on the last page.

This book is printed on acid-free paper.

Contents

Dedication

I dedicate this book to my son Rashan McMillan, my granddaughter Myaira McMillan My Mother Teddie Bradford who's deceased, family and friends.

Introduction

This story is being told to help others who have experienced the hurt and pain I have gone thru in my life as I traveled from church to church with a calling on my life. Once you have read my story it will help you on your journey in life. My story will give you a look at your own life and what you have gone thru. I will also help you to re-examine your surroundings and who you let become close to you. The hurt I felt and rejection may deliver you in a time of need, when things seem out of line and not on course. Reading my story may help you see the world thru a whole new pair of lenses. This will let you know you are not alone and it is possible to make it staying strong and determined.

Chapter 1

LIFE IN THE CHURCH - WOUNDED BUT YET WALKING

*L*ife has many avenues for us to go down which had me thinking there was safety in the church. Little did I know after spending some time there, and experiencing church people; have come to find out church people will hurt you. This is the least you would expect from church people. The church is supposed to be a place of safety, protection, healing and deliverance; not a place to be abused and attacked. It seemed to happen after my calling from God. One week there was a revival downtown in New Brunswick NJ on Haim Street. I attended the revival every night. I got down on our knees praying to Jesus each night. When the revival came to an end, I received the Holy Spirit and my life changed. I started to see God's creation in a whole new light and to appreciate His universe better. I was seeing thru a different pair of lenses. When the ushers picked me up that night everyone *looked at me seeing change. I began to praise God in a dance and was feeling good. The next day when people* saw me, they said you are born again! They were particular about how they dealt with me, there was greater respect. During my stay there in the church we had programs where ladies would play a part in the service. During the service there was some singing and some speaking. I couldn't sing so I spoke on

1

Naomi and Ruth in the Bible. I told how Naomi's husband died and Ruth went back with her mother in law to her home town. Ruth told her mother in-law your people will be my people and your God my God, wherever you go, I will go with you. Following her mother in law became a blessing and she married one of Naomi's relatives which was considered a "Kingsman redeemer" he was a rich man. I stayed at this church for a while and I wanted to do something to help the Pastor. This Pastor was instrumental in my newness in God and he prayed for me. I began planning and putting things into motion. I decided to have a program for him to raise money for the church. I reached out to the different singing groups and invited them to come sing on my program. I would be the MC of this program. I was able to advertise this event on the radio. The advertisement helped out a lot and was heard on WBLS radio station.

Advertising my program got the attention of a well-known MC. He came to meet me in person and gave some advice on how I could reach out more and make money being a MC. I was not interested in going that route. The Bible said freely you received and freely you give from my heart I put this program on. That night I was wearing a yellow chiffon dress with spits on the sleeves and a belt around the waistline. It was a very pretty dress from one of the boutiques I loved to shop in the mall. To start the program one of my preacher friends started with devotion followed by prayer, scripture and songs of Zion. The program started with me as MC introducing each group. The program was a success with all the groups showing up to sing for me. This event was an extra bonus to help with the fundraiser. I sold chicken dinners and chicken sandwiches at the end of the night with all proceeds going to the church. Once the program was over after several weeks went by I felt led to go back to my local church.

Chapter 2

MY LOCAL CHURCH

I returned to my local church and while there the Lord was dealing with me about calling for a revival so I begin to send out letters for speakers to come. I received a great response with a devotional leader included. I held a week revival with Ministers from Linden, NJ and Trenton, NJ. Every night was a success, people got born again. At the of the revival one of the ministers from Trenton, NJ asked who called this revival. I stood up and said I did; two of the ministers said God is sending you out to save souls. When I heard that I didn't understand but as time went on God revealed this meaning to me. I began to meet many people of all walks of life, praying for them and encouraging them. At that moment of time I started to travel to different churches helping out in devotion before the ministers arrived, so I wasn't at my church much. On my journey I met several Pastors, one night a play called the "Rapture" which was very heart felt, moved me. I took this play and returned to my home church to help bring the "Rapture" there. Before anything took place, they held a meeting concerning me and the role I played in the church. The church members informed me that I was not a paid member or a working member. I stood there listening, and it was very hurtful hearing those words. There's a calling on my life and I had to obey God's commission going out into the world to help others. In this church I paid my tithes and supported them putting on programs. When the meeting was over, I continued on with my program having a devotion first and then introducing the "Rapture," I stood strong in my place. God was sending me out on an assignment my time was up there.

Chapter 3

MY NEW ASSIGNMENT

I moved to my assignment at this new church which the Lord had led me to. Once I arrived was accepted has a new member along with my son who was good in church. He was accepted as a member in the choir, he sang better than the adult males and could remember a song to sing it. My son was so glad they no longer wanted him in the choir. It was my assignment, so we stayed one year and day. One Sunday, I spoke about going to a foreign country and how I met a Minister and the way God blessed me without paying anyone. Once the meeting was over the Overseer said I could never follow behind you again speaking because I was good. No matter how good I was they would not put me on the Missionary Board. The Pastor felt like the gift I had she needed in order to carry the church. I told her God has given each one of us the gift he wants us to have. At that moment, she felt as though if she didn't receive the gift I had; someone would take over the church. When we had meeting, I would try to talk to the people, but she wouldn't allow it. My presence was very moving with her people they appreciated the way I dealt with them being gentle not rough. The Pastor had a problem with treating the people gentle, so at times she wouldn't allow me to have any input on any situation in their life. Eventually God told her he sent an angel there and he was sending her back out because she didn't recognize her. Once God spoke to her she cried and later I left her church. This experience really had me seeking God more for my next move. When I arrived at the next Church would let the Pastor and church know I didn't come on my own but God setd me! A friend and I arrived at the next church, the Pastor and members knew God had sent m. They said that God had answered their prayer. The minute we got there they looked at me and my friend, the Pastor said bring them up front; and that was my seat from that day on. I continued to fellowship at the new Church as my friend Ms. Bee moved on. Time went by the Pastor said you're not only a Missionary but Evangelist. I joined the church and began to work in the ministry helping out at the altar as the Pastor prayed for people for deliverance and healing. On the first Sunday of the month, I was involved with communion which all the missionaries played a part. You would hold towels, the basin with water to wash their hands in or hold the container to collect the empty cups after communion was served. At this church there were times when my pastor would ask some of the missionaries to speak when my pastor didn't want to. This gave us an opportunity to exercise our gifts he was a fair Pastor and didn't mind sharing the ministry.

Chapter 4

MANY ARE CALLED BUT
FEW ARE CHOSEN

*A*t this church we had meeting with our pastor instruction us about our duties. Our church was very family oriented and I enjoyed that facet of it, meeting some new people and going to their houses until the next service on some Sundays. On some Sundays my Pastor would take all the missionaries out to dinner after church which I enjoyed. Once I was at the church for several months the pastor invited me to dinner with his wife at one of the member's house to get to know me better This gesture made me feel special. In this church the Missionaries where chosen by the pastor but I was one that was chosen and called by God to do a work for the Kingdom. In Church on Sundays my pastor would have one of the missionaries conduct devotion. I was chosen a lot of times because they said I had the gift to sing. This was an enjoyable time and once devotion was over sometimes, I was chosen to help with the offering. Missionaries on the fourth Sunday of every month had to speak and fifth Sunday we did the entire service and my Pastor made sure we had the opportunity to exercise our gifts. Our church had a great ministry of deliverance which the Lord used me greatly. One day my Pastor said I was one of his strongest missionaries that I had his back and didn't want me to leave. My Pastor knew I was there temporary and tried to keep me. God had sent me out on an assignment and to get my license which every missionary had to take a test to receive them. When the time came to take the test during our Holy Convocation, the head of the Missionary Board pulled me aside to tell me I couldn't take the test. She didn't have an explanation from my Pastor. This situation happened three times, so finally I addressed my Pastor to ask why and his response was he didn't want me to leave the church because I had his back. As time went on my spirit felt bound and I never forgot it. Once when I was wearing a hot pink dress with a bow tied in the back, this was during devotion time I got up to sing a song, "God has Smiled On Me and He has been good to me and He has set me free," at that moment I began to cry, my spirit was bound but I could feel the presence of the Lord begin free me again. I left the sanctuary to go to the bathroom and the mother of the church followed me asking "what's the matter?" I said my spirit was bound but now I am free. I was the second time I had gotten bound and had to get free! Once I was free, I left for a while without the license and stayed away for a while than later returned. Before I left, one of the members said she had a dream about a train crash and I was on the train, she said some men helped me get out. She said I was the only saint on the train and right after her dream I left the church. My Pastor told the member of the church that shared her dream that it meant I was going to leave. It was too much to deal with the different personalities', people are peculiar and mean. At the Altar, I would get attacked by three people telling me to "take your hand off that person" and saying "we don't need my help." This would hurt my feelings, so the next Sunday, I wouldn't work the altar then later they would ask for my help. I enjoyed working the altar seeing people's lives change. This seem to be a part of my calling and very effective. The other missionaries begin to see my gift in operation and got nasty attacking me often. I would pray about this situation because it hurt causing me to sit on Sundays rather than help.

When things like this happen, you get wounded until you're healed by God. Church hurt is the worst hurt in the world and it takes time to heal. I took the abuse for some time going out to visit other churches and visiting Hospitals to pray for the sick. "Wounded But yet walking" caused a whole new world to open for me to explore God open a door for me when the confusion started in the Church. I'd visit several Hospitals in my area and out of town the distance didn't matter. I would go in the rain, sleet or snow meeting very nice people. In my ministry, I would take clothes to the men's shelter to help when new men arrived. In my area, there are women shelters that I was instrumental in helping. I would take lotion and deodorant; this was part of my outreach ministry which I loved with no competition.

While at the church my Pastor would visit several churches with the congregation going with him, once we arrived my Pastor would tell the President of our missionary board to tell me to get prepared to speak. He chose me a lot when we went out to visit. My Pastor would send several of the missionaries out to other churches to speak getting us involved in collecting the offering and when the time came to give a response for the welcome address, they chose me, saying go ahead Sister McMillan and off I would go.

Chapter 5

OUTREACH MINISTRY

Wounded but yet walking as the battle goes on in the church, I confront my attackers asking why are you fighting me and their response was because you flow in the spirit and we don't. I had no idea what that meant, I was just obeying God and moving as He instructed me with the anointing to do the work. I continued to work at the altar and with the church being used of God. Finally, after being there seventeen years, God lead me out. I received my license from my New Pastor because the former one had passed away. The license was not just handed to me, I had to take a test. I received a ninety-five and was awarded my Evangelist licenses. I already had an outreach ministry which started from a vision God gave me. I saw myself laying hands on the sick this is when I started my outreach ministry sometimes one on one and other times someone would come along with as a team.

Once the hospital ministry started it led into a prison ministry from visiting some of the patient's family or friends. One of the patient's love one in prison and I was asked to take a care package. The day I went to visit, the journey was almost two hours and I got there too late so I had to go another day. That Tuesday I rested up and the next day started out again. Before I left the inmate mother's house, she gave me Fifty dollars.

I refused it but she insisted that I take it. I thank God I did because my battery went out so the Fifty dollars covered the battery.

This time I arrived on time visiting the inmate taking the care package and writing letters of encouragement, a ministry of helps. During this time, I was also asked to visit a mental institution. While I was there, a young lady saw me and said you are sunshine I have been waiting for you! She couldn't wait for the door to open, when I entered to visit. She said am going home now and left that place. There were several girls with nervous breakdowns from when they broke up with a boyfriend.

. My assignment was to pray for them, allow them to talk about what happened, giving out Bibles while visiting and sometimes Mrs. Administration would come along to help me. We would talk to the Girls and the Guys on the grounds while they were outside. I attended church on Sunday so I one Sunday went to pick up three young ladies from the institution. The young ladies had a wonderful time at church. Later I returned them to the institution, and finally they went home.

Once I left the church, I continued my outreach ministry waiting on my next assignment. I continued to visit other churches. One visit to my Church before leaving my Pastor said I see you leaving, we were standing in the back of the church close to the door going outside, I said "when you don't see me you will know I'm gone."

I can say I had a nice time fellowshipping serving in the ministry with my Pastor, deliverance and prayer for the saints. There was also the opportunity to help with communion on every fist Sunday. The Missionaries and Evangelist had the Fourth and Fifth Sunday which was our time to speak, allowing God to use us, at times it was our second service. I thank God for the time spent there but you really have to have tough skin to stand in the ministry because people in the church will attack you, everybody will not like you so you better have back up. I Thank God for my son and my mother they always had my back. When I went out to speak or to do my Hospital Ministry my son came along, he sees well in the spirit realm. One day, I was praying for a young lady when I touched her hand, on the other side my son saw a light come all around the both of us. This was the Sunday I spoke about Esther and how God used her to save her people, a woman who was not afraid to step up to the plate.

This was a beautiful move of God and a pleasure to have my son with me, nothing like having support. During this night, once I finish; the Deacon said to me "Mordecai was not her uncle," and I said "that's what the Bible said" and continued to greet the people. In life there seems to be a wolf larking around to discredit you but I stand on God's word.

The journey has not been an easy one, but God said "in this world you shall have tribulation" and I had no idea it would be in the church. I have experienced more hurt in the church then in the world, a place I thought would be a safe haven. It seems like, when you are in the midst and not being seen or heard; things are alright. Once your Ministry starts there is so much confusion and the wolves come out to stop you from doing the will of God.

I am a very sensitive person and I pick up a lot of stuff and feelings its part of my ministry, How can I know you're hurting, if I didn't feel your pain. In the ministry, the gift of discernment is needed for deliverance to come fourth and healing. The problem I had was being attacked while trying to help someone in need, that's pretty bad, especially when they are in ministry also, this is not Gods plan. That's why I guess Jesus had to steal away to pray and then come back in the cool of the day, by the time things had settled down.

I thank God for His example because in life that's what we have to do as humans, psalms 91 says; "he who dwells in the secret place of the most high shall abide under the shadow of the almighty."

Chapter 6

THE HIDING PLACE

There were times God had to hide me for the next move in him. During this time, God Is giving you more strength for the next task. You are "wounded yet walking" because there is a job to be done that, he has called you to, so gird you up your loins to move again.

In Psalms 23, He tells us "He is our shepherd and our guide," putting goodness and mercy beside us as we walk. He is there to hold us up so we can continue this race set before us. The road has been rough and if it wasn't for the love of God and accepting Jesus into my life, I wouldn't even go to church, but I love fellowshipping and I love the Lord.

My main focus is to help those in need, the rejected the down hearted and the abandoned, to be able to minister to them. I have gone to church all my life from a little girl, to a Baptist church and Pentecostal church. I love the move of God, the Holy Spirit working on people, when in this mode I am in my glory. "Wounded but yet walking," helping others get delivered. Let me tell you how sweet God is, he saw me being attacked and opened up a door for a Hospital Ministry which I enjoyed praying for the sick and reading God's word.

At times I would listen to their story and allow them to tell me how their day went which was healing to the patient.

At times, someone might need me in the middle of the night and I would go, I wanted to always be available. During this time of visitation, I would meet patients that had love ones in prisons and I would be asked to visit them taking care packages, it was a one on one ministry praying for them before I left.

There was no distance I would go to help and at times they would try to pay me but I said "no" freely I received the gift from God and freely I give to you. There was one exception, this one time, I had to go to a prison two hours away and the mother said take this $50.00. I said no but she insisted, thank God she did because my battery stopped working and the fifty dollars was a blessing it paid for the battery so I continued on my journey to see her son.

On this assignment there were clothes that needed to be delivered and food so I was able to accomplish everything. Then there came a time when I was needed to visit a mental institution for several young ladies that had broken up with boyfriends. I would pray and fast before going and once I arrived at the institution, would pray with them and talk about how they felt and gave out Bibles. This went on for a while until they were able to return home. On one Sunday, I went to pick up three of the young ladies taking them to my church.

I have seen God's hand move many people and I love one on one ministry, there is no one to attack you, just you and God and that individual who's so glad to see you cared enough to come see about them.

God is still on the throne and has not forgotten His people, we have to continue to walk and do the work He has called us to, even in our wounded hour. It was time to spread my wings again, after leaving the church I had been in for seventeen years. I began to evangelize again, going to visit other churches, having speaking engagements and attending college. I worked in the day time and went to college at night for about three hours on Tuesdays and Thursdays to get my Master Degree in Counseling which I accomplished. This was something God had laid on my heart because I saw so many wounded and hurt people in the church, plus I myself was one of them, so the class was very beneficial to me while interacting with other students.

Chapter 7

STAYING IN THE RACE

Sometimes in life we get a blow and wonder if we can get back up. We ask: Lord will I stand again? The things I use to do before being wounded, will I do again? The church has a way of wounding you to the point of no return. One finds themselves at a lost, what did I do wrong to deserve this treatment from the Bishop or Co – Pastor, or Missionary? The church is supposed to be a safe haven not a battle ground where you attack God's love ones.

In the church, over the years I have experience jealousy in the church. As long as you sit and do nothing, people are satisfied but the minute the gifts are in operation there is a shift in the atmosphere.

I preached at this church but one thing they wouldn't do was to put me on the missionary board. That didn't stop me, I continued to fellowship with the church operating in an outreach ministry. There was time when some of the members had been missing church, so on Saturday morning I would visit their homes. The visits would be prayer, talk, and by the time my visit was over they would say" I'll see you at church Sunday." There wasn't a close contact with everyone but I tried to interact with the people. The Pastor wouldn't allow me to get to know the people. The congregation felt I was gentle with them. There was a time that we spoke, she told me the gift that I had; and she needed it or somebody else would take over the church. I informed her that God gives each of us gifts He wants us to have and she could not have mine.

The day came for me to preach and the overseer spoke after me. I had taken a trip to Haiti and all I wanted was peace and my confidence back, so I spoke on my trip. In, Haiti we went up into the mountains for church and the Minister asked how would I like to be a missionary? My reply to the Minister was, I don't know if I have to come this far. During my visit to Haiti, I received my peace and confidence for free and didn't have to pay anyone. When I came back, *felt free and confident. This message troubled the overseer and she said you were too good and I will never come after you again.*

That didn't move me but after that the Lord sent me out. The Lord spoke to the Pastor telling her telling her; "I sent an angel here but you weren't aware of her so I'm sending her ou.t" The Pastor cried and me and my son left. During the time at the church, my son was very instrumental in the choir he could remember a song better than the men singing. One day they decided my son was no longer wanted in the choir, it was a low blow. When I left that church. I prayed to God that the next time he sends me out; let them know He sent me. My next assignment, God did just that, he proved himself to me. The minute they saw me, the pastor said" bring her up front" and they sat me and a friend in the front row.

In life we go thru many changes, we didn't get a road map when we started on this journey. We have no idea what will happen or how we will be treated by others. The Bible says; we shall have tribulation, but I had no way of knowing it concerned the mistreatment of people in the church. I look at the church as a sanctuary, a safe haven, a place of shelter, a loving place.

There have been obstacles put in my way because of the gift that came from God my creator. When others don't operate on the same level as you, they seem to have a problem with you. On this journey you don't have to bother anyone they can just see you operate in the gift and the wolf comes out for the attack. I guess that's why the Lord put this verse in the Bible about "wolves in sheep clothing." He told us to be aware of them, but I was trying to love everybody and be nice even when I was being attacked. The word of God says in Ephesians the six chapter to put on the whole armor of God to fight the good fight of faith. He said our weapons are not carnal but are mighty in pulling down the strongholds. We need the sword of the spirit to cut the devil as they come to attack us, the sword cuts two ways not one. It's important to have our head covered with the helmet of salvation. I often heard the mature saints say to cover your head, they had a reason. The breast plate of righteousness covers your front, and our feet shod with the preparation of the Gospel. It's important to know the Word of God so in times of a fight you can speak it, "no weapon formed against me shall prosper and I am more than a conquer in Christ Jesus."

In the new church the Pastor said he knew God had sent me so the word backed me up. The pastor saw who I was, not only a Missionary but an Evangelist and he had no problem putting me on the Missionary Board.

My opportunity came to speak on the fourth Sunday and sometimes the fifth. The deliverance work was a gift from God I would move and say what the Holy Spirit told me to say. It was a pleasure working with the Pastor having his back, but at times the devil would creep into three people while God was using me on the altar, they seemed to be strategically planted and knew when to attack.

They would hit my arm and say, "she doesn't need your help" and the second one would say; "take your hand off her." As I came down the aisle the third one would be waiting for me. This was all new to me and I didn't know how to deal with it. There was a young lady in the church and she was very nice and she told me I had to fight back, she even told them to back up and leave me alone.

In time, incidents like these wound and hurt, not getting up to help. I always believe in being nice to others, not nasty, if you would have told me church people will hurt you, I would not have believed you. When you have had church hurt that's the worse hurt in the world hard to shake it off. This type of hurt you carry with you no matter where you go, like a scar on your body people can't see it but it's still there. There comes a time when you will, you have to take a stand and tell them to back up; "I am Gods property and don't put your hands on me anymore."

God has to shield us from the enemy that's why people wear certain garments, you see how they dress for war. That's how God's people have to be, His servants must arm themselves for the battle. We must fight the good fight of faith to stay in the race set before us or we will be a wounded soldiers looking for someone to bandage our wounds. During my time of struggle, I can say the following Sunday, I sat down there came a time they needed my help and called on me to come deliver someone. If they were on the floor God gave me the right word to get them off. Dealing with spiritual things sometimes people get afraid not knowing what's happening to them. This the time God needs his servants to be on post and wise counselors. This is where I came in, God would instruct me on how to deal with an individual.

When you're wounded, you must regroup to complete your assignment. There are times God will put you in a hiding place until he wants to bring you back out again. My favorite Psalms is 91, he that dwells in the secret place of the Most High, shall abide under the shadow of the almighty. We have to find a dwelling place; there you find peace in the Holy Ghost. In this place God will refill you replenishing you for the next assignment. While your dwelling there, He wipes away some of the hurt pouring oil and wine into your wounds, as the Good Samaritan did to the man that got robbed on the back road to Damascus. God will take care of you because He still has work for you to do, wounded one.

The pain that people experience, what better person to help then the one who has been wounded. They know the pain and the heartache you have been going through. We all have gifts for a purpose and sometimes question them, but they are for the work of the ministry.

One of my greatest gifts is sensitivity, which I use to hate but later found out it was needed for the ministry. At times you might want to hide but God is still on the throne and He's not finished with us.

It has been an uphill battle and I have learned a lot even when I am wounded, that might have been a time to be still while God heals me. I love the Lord and if he hadn't called me to the ministry, I probably would have sat down a long time ago. There have been times I was wounded but still continued to walk, wounded and still visiting the sick in the hospital. Wounded but still visiting the man in prison and the woman in the mental institution.

When we are wounded, we have to remember there might be somebody worse off then you, so don't stop. We all have a destiny to reach and if you stop you might not never get there. I can also remember an animal licking his wounds until it got healed and back up again. He did not stay in that condition long.

Being wounded hurts but thank God for being a healer as I write today, it doesn't feel so bad. I believe somethings are behind me and I can run on to see what the end is going to be. There is victory in Jesus and He heals all our wounds.

Chapter 8

CONQUERED LIFE

*O*ur lives are built to conquer all things, so during your time of being wounded it's important to keep praying for strength. It's important to keep on walking even though you are wounded. To get to your next destination you must keep moving. When you're wounded its hurts and you don't feel like doing anything, but remember you are a survivor and made in God's image. In your wounded time, know you're made by God He created you not man.

It's hard to work in the church when you're wounded, all you can think about is how you feel. There is an old saying; "sticks and stones may hurt my bones but words may never hurt me" that's not true words do hurt. The word you hear they are carried along with you wherever you go. Once you put a word out there you can't take it back, so be careful how you speak to one another.

In this world you can wound someone for life and not even know it. Its 2020 and we are going into another year and are looking forward to a newness in God. There comes a time for healing to take place in our lives, healing takes time it doesn't always come over night. We have to go thru the process.

Being wounded is something you carry with you. The wounded may not show the scar on the body but it's there deep inside your body.

I can say the heart aches and the mind thinks why they treated me like this, I was only trying to help. There are gifts people see in you that you don't even see in yourself and they get in an attack mold. I believe the right Godly thing would be to work together. The church is the body of Christ not an individual. The gifts are given to edify the church so no one should get jealous of another and attack. Being in the church and called by God I have learned a lot of lessons. When I was young it wasn't like today. The spirit wound move in the church and people got delivered with no competition, the church was family oriented it had standards. Once I got my calling in 1978 and began to travel all hell broke loose. The world didn't treat me like the church did attacking me while working in the church. My job is to help people to get set free and renew their sprit. The spirit is the only thing going back to God when we leave this body. The body is a vehicle to house the spirit. I have met many people in darkness not knowing about God and how they had to be renewed, Psalms 51 says; "create in me a clean heart and renew in me the right spirit." When we are renewed by God and having the fruit of the Spirit, He will teach you how to love one another not hurt.

Why would someone want to hurt another person when they haven't done them any harm, well I can say I got my answer from my attackers after asking the question. The response I got was, you flow in the spirit and I don't. My answer was, don't blame me it's a gift from God. God equips us with everything He wants us to have for the ministry. If you don't have what someone else has, stay humble and work with what you have. God will exalt you in do season. In this world, everyone has a season; spring, summer, fall and winter. God has a master plan for our timing when our season will change but wait on him. We must wait for our appointed time to come and not go ahead of God.

`   We all have dreams and visions, hold unto them they will come to pass, always remember you may be wounded but God still wants to use you. The pain and the heartache the wounded person have gone thru can help others in the same situation. There is a place for you in the kingdom of God, so make your mark wounded one. It's time to rise and shine for the battle is not yours but the Lord. The wounded

ones are still apart of God's army; he will put the whole armor upon you so you can fight the good fight of faith.

The shield is there to cover your body with the sword of the spirit in your hand, God's breast plate of righteousness and your feet shod with the preparation of the gospel and the helmet of salvation. Always have your armor on and be prepared for the battle, you will never know where the enemy may be lurking around.

Chapter 9

THE HEALING PROCESS

*T*he weapons of our warfare are not carnal but mighty in pulling down the strongholds. When you're wounded, there is a time for the bandages to go on, but then there comes a time to take them off for the healing process to be completed. In my ministry, I have had followers for a short time, there were some ministering in the hospitals and other times a track ministry. At times a minister friend would accompany me to the mental institution to visit patients, taking Bibles and praying for them to be healed.

Later there was an extension to my ministry of visiting the sick, I met love ones who had someone in prison so I extended myself to visit them. This visit consisted of me taking care packages which would be clothing and when I didn't visit, I would write to encourage them, and later the shelters were added with me taking deodorant and lotion to the women. During the week, it was important to take under garments to the men's shelter. There were so many people coming in there, it was a need to make sure they had enough and it was appreciated.

Wounded but yet walking, be clothed for the battle because it's hard to fight when you're wounded. You must keep moving while you are healing. In the army, soldier's bandage their wounds but keep their weapon in hand and proceed to fight the enemy. In life, there comes a time, we have to rid ourselves of what's holding us back. When you're wounded, it's a hard blow, the hit seems to knock you down and one doesn't seem to have the fight they use to have.

When I first was called, I had a zeal for God like none other, once the blow came, I felt like setting down in Church. There came a time, I had to regroup before getting back up again. One thing I can say, if you have ever had church hurt, it's the worse hurt in the world. This type of pain goes deep into the core. The type of pain that makes you cry even thinking about the words spoken. It also makes you sad, you carry the pain everywhere you go and once you think about what happened you cry.

Chapter 10

WHEN PAIN TURNS TO TEARS

The scab comes off a sore but if you pick it, you won't heal; that's how words are, they cut deep into the spirit and soul of a person. I found it hard to work in the church, there is a spirit of jealousy that cuts. God said; "with love and kindness I have drawn thee!" We are supposed to love one another and to encourage each other.

The body is to work for the building of God's kingdom, we are not to tear each other down, but to build up its rough. I enjoy doing outreach ministry because inside building there is problems and conflict with people. I have found outreach ministry to be the most rewarding of all. The outreach ministry covers a lot of territory, such as Hospitals, prisons, mental institutions, and shelters. God gave His disciples a great commission to go out into all the world to reach those that were lost, feeding the hungry, clothing those naked, and healing the sick.

There are people to be healed, delivered and set free, we live in a world where people are hurting not only outside the church but inside. I remember I was hurting but my pastor didn't know until I told him. One Sunday I felt so bad I just began to cry and had to speak to him.

My authority to pray for people came from God. As an Evangelist called by God, working in the church, my Pastor gave me permission to pray for the people. Having the permission from the Pastor didn't stop the attacks, they continued. While in my Pastor's office, he told me to stop crying before I make him cry; I finally composed myself and left his office. My Pastor instructed me on what to say to the next person that might try to stop me. Things went on smooth after bringing my problem to my Pastor then my time at the church finally came to an end and my assignment was up.

Chapter 11

WOUNDED BUT YET WALKING

Our lives are built to conquer all things thru Christ Jesus! In our time of being wounded, it's important to keep walking even though you are wounded. To get to your next, you must keep moving. When you are wounded, it hurts and you don't feel like doing anything but remember you are a survivor and made in God's image. In this world you can wound someone for life and not even know it.

Its 2020 and we are about to go into another year I am looking forward to a newness in God. There comes a time for the body of Christ to act as the body of Christ not an individual. In my wounded time, God leads me to a place of safety to continue fellowshipping and during this time I gain strength for the next assignment. While in the appointed church, I still speak and do deliverance all for the glory of God. There were times God gave me a song for someone in the church that would minister to their spirit, I would say that's your song it's for you.

My God never stopped using me even thou I was wounded and hurt that's way I like Psalms 91, "He that dwells in the secret place of the Most High shall abide under the shadow of the almighty." God has a secret place for his wounded ones, a hiding place where we have to make it to that place, molded by our creator in order to get to the high place in Him. There is a high place He wants to take us and people get in the way but God keeps pushing us higher and higher. We have to find the power within us to never stop, no matter what and to keep running. I remember when I was in the nursing unit for the state of New Jersey I was called the flying nun, I was so involved in everything and going to different events and churches with such a free spirit.

I worked with the funeral homes; I would stand by the casket as the families proceeded in line to encourage them. When someone fainted, I was there to help them wake up by just calling their name. There came a time that you couldn't use smelling salt anymore. When it was time to travel in New York for visiting a church, I lead the way. During the service, if you needed someone to respond to the welcome address, I was chosen. There were times I was asked to MC a program and other times to speak.

At one church, I was on the hospitality club, willing workers, trustee, financial secretary and helping with the offering every Sunday. In this church, I was responsible for giving a quarterly report concerning the church's affairs and our finances This was a job well done, if I must say so myself. I also brought in programs to raise money for the church, even thou I got cheated out of one of them never getting credit.

I remained steadfast knowing God is still on the throne, wounded but yet walking, at the moment am helping out which I love. This Church is peaceful and the Pastor is wonderful, I am on the Women's another church Committee and Hospitality.

Chapter 12

WORKING AND MINISTRY

One of the most pleasant things I like is hospitality serving others, when I visit the hospital, return home so full joy, giving all the glory to God. In this place the people appreciate you for taking a moment out of your schedule to visit them. It could be just a simple question finding out how their day went. In Pastoral care, a patient would say; oh my Pastor came by and I would say that's a blessing and we continued to talk praying for their need.

I know God has something great for me, I haven't gone thru all this hurt and pain for nothing; there is greatness waiting for me and those wounded ones out there. When I read the Bible, Paul talks about how he was ship wrecked, hurt, how people labored with him in the Gospel, other times no one helped. He was abandoned and still one of God's disciples.

"Wounded but yet walking," now what about the wounded ones, sounds like we are having a Paul's experience. I'm looking for the greatness, the latter shall be greater than the former. A Prophet said to me, when I was first called, that God would use me in my latter years.

While doing ministry, I was working in a large technical school and in charge of the Data Entry department. I would put the information in for the students and some of the office work. In this job, I made all the programs to input data, plus ran all the reports. It was at the end of the year and a shift came to bring in new supervisors. It was close to my time for drawing on social security and you aren't allowed to make over a stated amount, so I left.

This experience made me feel bad, but before I left, a friend took me out for lunch and then back to my office; there was a party for me. Once I entered the room, I began to cry; there stood all my coworkers celebrating me. They brough gifts for me with the Bible verse Romans 8:28; letting me know this was working for my good. The verse said, "all things work together for the good of those that are called according to His purpose.

I couldn't see it then but there was a friend that needed my help. He was sick, so once I left the job was able to help him. It consisted of me taking him to the doctor, making sure he had meals every day and handling his business properly. This gave me more time to work for God lending a helping hand. In my wounded time of walking with God, I learned that there were gifts in me that I never knew about. One of the gifts was exhortation which I didn't do with a loud voice but the people got the message. I also learned from the Biblical profile, that I showed mercy and it's true; my heart goes out to hurting people, those that are forgotten or wounded.

When they can't find anyone else to help them, I'll step in to deliver them. I can say I am a server in many capacities in the church with Hospitality and visiting the hospital. In the home, with those that are bound or even in the prison, taking those that may need a care package. My heart is big and I try to help out wherever there is a need. In my travels. I've learned; I am a rescuer, I saw a need and felt lead to perform it. One day I heard a healer on the Radio from Chicago, he was coming to New York City; so, I made plans to go see him. There was a young lady going out of Hillside so we drove together. A healing seminar was held by this renowned healer with lunch being served.

Once the lunch was over, I met several healers and authors calling me to the stage for everyone to pray for me. The healer in charge, wanted me to help him as he prayed for the people, as they laid hands on me; I saw a bright light and it got brighter. This is the first time I felt so light. It was very fulfilling as I stood, the people looked at me. One of the TV stars from a popular show said, thanks for bringing us the light. Then I walked off the stage and began to pray for the people as the spirit of God led me. The first thing I had to do, was walk with the healer from Chicago and then on my own. What a wonderful time and at end of the service people were coming behind me to pray for them. In this service there was such a peace in the room. That week I received a call from the healer I worked with at the seminar. He said, you are a rescuer but you can't rescue everybody and everybody doesn't want to be rescued. I thought about what he said and continued to help people. One thing I did learn, was to slow down and not run so much.

There came a time when I almost burned myself out, between working a full-time job, taking care of my son and doing my ministry. In our busy times, we learn from experience, which is the best teacher. When I woke up this morning and started reading some of the work which was done in my leadership class, it showed how Esther had a mentor, her uncle, to guide her and how she was instrumental in saving her people. Then there was Deborah and how her parents were instrumental in teaching her, being a mentor in every step of her life.

Chapter 13

LEARNING FROM THE ANIMAL KINGDOM

When I look at Deborah, she was one that didn't play with the enemy, her name means bee, and she was busy fulling her duties dealing with the enemy when they attacked her.

Quote: "Science confirms the ancient belief that out of all the animal kingdom the bee was among the highest in intelligence says Mary Hal let," so Deborah stands out as among the wisest of all the Old Testament women. This is a woman that all women can learn from, she was gifted with superior spiritual, mental and physical power, a woman of great power born to rule.

"Wounded but yet walking;" I saw this woman as an example in the Bible, one that can help you to suit up and to fight the good fight of faith. It's important to help to look at an example that will help you to stand in your time of pain rather than give up and be still. This woman allowed you to see what others have gone thru, survive the test and the assignment that has been given to them. In this life, many curve balls can be thrown to you but it's important to keep moving. The pain is powerful and real, sometimes hard to shake off. This kind of pain you seem to carry no matter what, you want to let it go but it's a pain and a wound that takes time.

When you're wounded, God has to heal you, bandages come on for a certain period of time, then they must be removed so the sore can heal. There is a story in the Bible I like to tell you about, the man from Jerusalem on the road to Jericho and who fell among thieves they robbed him of his raiment and left him for dead. Sometimes we think a person is our friend but when the going gets stuff, they begin to get lost, but true friends will stick around.

Let me tell you what happened on that road, a Levite came, then a priest and went to the other side but a good Samaritan came and put the man on his horse. He took him to an inn pouring oil and wine in his wounds to heal him. Don't just leave your loved ones when hard times come but help them up, have compassion and humility. When you are wounded, you find out just who your friends are and you feel left alone. It's during this moment, you have time to reflect on your life, to find out your next move. The way you have done things in the past will change, being wounded, helps you to take a long look at life and how you feel right now. In the next assignment, you will become more watchful and protecting yourself from the enemy. The word of God says, to put on the whole amour of God, Ephesian's 6. We have to be equipped, it's important to cover our bodies with the armor of God. May you be blessed by my story and I hope it will help someone to heal while being wounded but yet walking.

Printed in the United States
By Bookmasters